Hidden Treasures

LOUISE DUPONT

Order this book online at www.trafford.com
or email orders@trafford.com

Most Trafford titles are also available at major online book retailers.

© Copyright 2012 Louise Dupont.

All rights reserved. No part of this publication may be reproduced, stored in a retrieval system, or transmitted, in any form or by any means, electronic, mechanical, photocopying, recording, or otherwise, without the written prior permission of the author.

Book designer: Brigitte Rosenlund

Cover photo: Marc Gallant/Winnipeg Free Press, Feb. 15, 2003, reproduced with permission

Adapted from "Prayer for Our Children", from ILLUMINATA by Marianne Williamson, copyright © 1994 by Marianne Williamson. Used by permission of Random House, Inc.

Printed in Canada.

ISBN: 978-1-4669-2269-3 (sc)
ISBN: 978-1-4669-9656-4 (e)

Library of Congress Control Number: 2012905598

Trafford rev. 01/31/2014

 www.trafford.com

North America & international
toll-free: 1 888 232 4444 (USA & Canada)
phone: 250 383 6864 ♦ fax: 812 355 4082

Acknowledgments

I would like to thank:

Brigitte Rosenlund, my book designer, who helped me bring this book to life;

The staff at the *Winnipeg Free Press* for allowing me to use the picture on the cover of this book;

Jeannette Fillion-Rosset, who encouraged me to embark on this journey;

Janine Tougas and Satori Diop, who took me under their wings for the first part of this journey;

Jeff Staflund, Julie Gautron, Liliane and Robert Régnier, Noella Rouire, Janelle Trudel, Elaine Tougas, Rick Puteran, Ron Sigurdson, Vivianne Roy Mazerolle and Hilda Wyenberg;

The following students of École Christine-Lespérance, who gave me permission to use their cards/drawings: Claudine Gauvin, Danica Knockaert, Daniel Bouchard, Dominic Beaulieu, Rebecca Ricard, Katie Miller, Véronique Cormier and Justin Patenaude;

All those who read the manuscript and gave me their feedback.

To Ephrem, Nathalie and Christian,

André's many friends,

and the students of École Christine-Lespérance

God answers sharp and sudden on some prayers and thrusts the thing we have prayed for in our face. A gauntlet with a gift in it.

Elizabeth Barrett Browning

My intention...

My initial goal, as I started this project, was to bring to a wider audience a symbolic and inspiring story my son had written. As I progressed along this path, it became a vehicle through which I could talk about depression and my son's suicide. It allowed me to share my journey towards healing and reconciliation. It is also my hope that this book will help to spark a discussion about these difficult topics.

While writing, I was guided by two overriding principles. Since suicide takes such an emotional toll on everyone involved, I was determined to write a book that was uplifting and healing in nature. It was also very important to me that this work be a reflection of my son's gentle and inquisitive spirit.

As I open my heart, I invite you to open yours and follow me on this journey where you will surely find some hidden treasures...

Louise Dupont

ANDRÉ DUPONT
October 24, 1981 — April 6, 2003

After my death, I will let fall a shower of roses.
I will spend my heaven doing good upon earth.

Thérèse de Lisieux

André, cycling in the heart of North America –
on the plains of Manitoba

I discover a hidden treasure...

In April 2004, a year after my 21-year-old son, André, had committed suicide, I was looking for his graduation pictures, when I happened to find a story that he had written in elementary school. André would have been seven years old at the time this story was written.

It comes from the heart of the North American continent, in Winnipeg, Manitoba, Canada. I wanted to share this tale because it speaks of love and hope. It is rich in symbols and inspiring messages.

Since the beginning of time, man has pursued happiness and searched for the meaning of life. Along with the subject of healing, these themes have always been of great interest to me. I believe the following tale is a good example of these quests.

André was in Grade 2 at École Lavallée when he wrote this short story. His teachers, Mrs. Lorette Delaquis and Ms. Sylvie Guérard, put a great deal of emphasis on developing their students' French writing skills. The students were all given the same title, *Lost in the Storm*, and from there had to imagine a story.

This is what my son wrote...

Perdu dans la tempête

Lost in the Storm

André Dupont

Un beau jour je me promenais dans la forêt. Tout d'un coup des gros flocons de neige tombaient du ciel.

One fine day I was walking in the forest.
Suddenly, big snowflakes started falling from the sky.

Je ne pouvais rien voir autour de moi. Je voulais retourner à la maison mais j'étais perdu parce-que j'avais marché dans le mauvais sens.

I couldn't see anything around me. I wanted to go home but I was lost because I had walked in the wrong direction.

Que faire? Quand je cherchais pour ma maison j'ai vu une espèce d'animal.

What should I do? While I was looking for my house, I saw some kind of animal.

c'était un fantôme de lumière. Il était tout brillant

It was a ghost made of light. He was all shiny.

I followed him. All of a sudden, I saw my house.

J'ais couruu vite à la maison. J'étais très content de retourner à la maison.

I quickly ran to the house. I was glad to be home.

Mais avant de rentrer j'ai aperçu que j'étais à la mauvaise maison. Un monsieur a dit: "Donne moi tout ton argent et je vais te ramener à la maison."

But before I entered, I realized that I was at the wrong house. A man said: "Give me all your money and I will take you home."

I said I had no money. "O.K."

Alors il faudra que tu ailles dans ce labyrinthe et quand tu auras fini tu vas te trouver à la maison.

"Then you will have to enter this labyrinth and when you are finished you will find your house."

"Vas y." J'ai été dans le labyrinthe.

"Go ahead." I entered the labyrinth.

Je ne trouvais pas la fin. Tout à coup j'ai vu le fantôme de lumière.

I couldn't find my way out. All of a sudden, I saw the ghost made of light.

Il m'a dit que si je suivais un mur je me rendrais à la fin. J'ai fait qu'est ce qu'il m'a dit. Quand j'étais à la fin j'étais à la maison.

He told me that if I followed a wall it would lead me to the end. I did what he told me to do. When I got to the end, I was home.

J'étais content,

I was happy.

Here are some photos André took when he travelled in Europe...

Taken in the French Alps, this majestic scenery reminds me of André's open and adventurous spirit. He had a keen interest in discovering the world around him.

Solitude and freedom come to mind as I look at this picture, taken in Spain. André must have experienced many moments of solitude in his short life. His bicycle, a constant companion, most certainly provided him many moments of freedom.

A portrait of André's life...

The moment André entered the world he was surrounded by people who loved him: parents, grandparents, aunts, uncles and cousins. All were there to encourage and support him at different stages of life.

As a child, André had a vivid imagination. He enjoyed creating imaginary worlds with his tiny Smurfs and was adept at building elaborate structures with his Construx toys. Watching Passe-Partout, a televised puppet show, was the highlight of his day. He loved books and I would often find him curled up on his dad's knees, reading one of his favourite stories.

André had his faults and did present us with a few challenges while growing up. At times he made some poor decisions. When this happened, he would own up to his mistakes and learn some very valuable lessons.

By the age of 21, my son had grown into a generous and open-minded young man. Always curious, he wanted to learn all he could about the world. After completing high school, he travelled twice to Europe where he cycled through France, Spain and Italy. Eager to explore Manitoba, he often went cycling out in the countryside. One day, upon his return from such an excursion, having missed my birthday, he brought me a bouquet of grass and wild flowers he had picked. This precious moment, filled with so much tenderness, is forever etched in my memory and in my heart.

Marianne

André played hockey with the St-Vital Victorias (1996-1997)

André always gave one hundred percent when playing any sport. I admired his passion and energy as well as his commitment to the teams he played on.

André was an avid cyclist. In winter and in summer he would be pedaling his way around St. Boniface or St. Vital. One morning, as I was getting ready for work, he asked if he could borrow my bicycle. It was an old model that I had recently purchased. For some reason André was quite intrigued by it. That evening, as I was coming home from work, a gentle rain was falling outside and there out on the street was André pedaling my bicycle very nonchalantly. He took his time, not a care in the world, oblivious to the fact that he would soon be drenched to the bones.

One day he took part in a bicycle rally with couriers who deliver mail in Winnipeg. It was a scavenger or treasure hunt of sorts. He was instructed to go to different locations in the city to find clues that would lead him to the next stop. He was competing against couriers who knew the city very well and who were in great physical condition because they spent their days cycling as part of their work.

André won the race. I will never forget his excitement at having achieved this feat. He told me that he thought he had won the race because he had taken a few moments before jumping onto his bicycle to study the map that had been provided to the competitors before the start of the rally. By studying the map beforehand, he knew exactly where he was going and therefore wasted less time at each stop. This strategy allowed him to win the race.

André had a passion for languages and other cultures. French was his mother tongue and as a child, he quickly learned English. In high school, he had the opportunity to learn Spanish and would later learn Italian. He often sought out opportunities to speak and become more proficient in these languages. He had a keen interest in all kinds of music. He shared these interests with his sister, Nathalie, with whom he had forged a close relationship.

Sports were an important part of André's life. When he played hockey, soccer, volleyball, lacrosse or ultimate Frisbee, it was always with passion and determination. His participation in all these sports helped him to develop his leadership skills. As well, he was an avid soccer and hockey fan. There were many animated conversations about his favourite hockey team, *Les Canadiens de Montréal*, when he was with his cousins and uncles.

In high school he learned how to juggle and began playing hacky sack. These quickly became his preferred hobbies. He became a skilled juggler, in part, because he had an excellent partner, his younger brother Christian. They spent countless hours honing their skills while enjoying each other's company.

Wanting to share this passion with others, André had organized a juggling club for the students at École Christine-Lespérance where he worked as an educational assistant. The students really enjoyed being a part of this club.

My son had a wide circle of friends. He had the ability to forge friendships wherever he went. He loved to go winter camping with some of these friends and he never passed up the chance to play cards or board games.

In November of 2002, André visited the International Centre, where he met and quickly became friends with a newly arrived family of Columbian refugees. He started to visit them, helped them set up their apartment and taught them English. André spent one of his last weekends at the hospital helping his friend, Ronald, after an operation. André was able to use his interpretation skills to help Ronald and his family communicate with the doctors.

Here is André with his Colombian friends (from left to right) – Ronald, Nancy, José Jimenez. I was surprised to see that he was very open and curious about other cultures since he had not been raised in a multi-cultural environment.

André always wore his famous red cap. This picture was taken at Aikens Lake where he was fishing with some friends. He was very lucky to have caught such a big fish. I imagine, though, that he did not always feel so lucky.

I worry about my son's health...

André's last few years of life were quite difficult. Before leaving on his second trip to Europe, he seemed a bit melancholy and preoccupied. I later learned that he had been informed by his girlfriend that he could meet her in France but that she would no longer be his girlfriend. He later told us that this trip had been a disaster from start to finish. In Italy, where he started his trip, he had difficulty accessing his money. In the mountains, he encountered snowstorms that made cycling almost impossible. Arriving in France, he had hoped to convince his ex-girlfriend to resume their relationship, but to no avail. Since his plans were now in turmoil, he took refuge at his friend Alain's for a few days and came home to Canada much earlier than planned.

He seemed so different when he came home from that trip. He was no longer the confident young man we used to know. He spent a lot of his time sleeping and watching television. This was very unusual for André. He saw less and less of his friends. In hindsight, it seems that André did not have the tools to cope with the ending of an important relationship. This and many other factors caused him to sink more deeply into despair. I remember one evening at suppertime. We were all sitting around the table and I could see André pushing pieces of meat around his plate. He seemed so discouraged. I quickly went to the bathroom to hide my tears. At times, he seemed to bounce back and regain some of his energy. At one point, he did go for counseling but he did not want to see a doctor or any other professional who could have helped him.

I understood André's anguish and despair as I had also suffered from depression for many years. I knew that he struggled to just make it through each day. Not knowing what to do to help him or where to turn for help, I would often read a prayer by Marianne Williamson:

Dear God,
There are no words for the depth of my love for this child. I pray for his care and his protection. I surrender him into Your hands. Please, dear God, send Your angels to bless and surround him always.

In one of our last conversations, André questioned me about the war in Iraq, which had just been declared. He seemed very troubled by this event. It was as if he was carrying the weight of the world on his shoulders.

The storm begins...

Monday, April 7, 2003 started like any other day but did not end that way. Upon my return from work, my husband Ephrem announced that he had received a call from a teacher at École Christine-Lespérance telling him that André had not shown up for work that day. Trying not to panic, we decided that Ephrem would go to St. Boniface College that evening to see if he could find André's bicycle. We were hoping he would attend his evening class. As I waited for Ephrem's return, I started making some phone calls. Desperately trying to hold back the tears, I called some of André's friends to see if they knew where he was. I also called some family members and asked them to come and help us look for him. That same morning, my sister-in-law had seen an article in the newspaper about a young man who had been hit by a truck on the Perimeter Highway, not that far from home. I called the police detachment and was informed that the officer in charge of that case had gone home for the evening and to call back the next day. Knowing that this would be a long, sleepless night, I took a sweater that André always wore and huddled onto the couch with it.

It was an endless night. I knew that the next morning I would have to make that call to the police officer. I was certain my husband would be unable to perform this dreaded task. Around nine o'clock I called the officer telling him that our son had disappeared and that we were wondering if the young man mentioned in the newspaper could be him. After I had answered all his questions, he told me that he would call us back as soon as he had any news.

Later that afternoon the police officer came to tell us that André was indeed the young man in question. He explained that André had gone to Maple Grove Park in St. Vital where he had started to slit his wrists. Someone walking their dog had interrupted him. Since he was very determined to end his life, he had headed out on foot to the Perimeter Highway nearby. Hiding behind a cement abutment, he had then jumped in front of a five-ton truck that was coming down the road.

I remember being very calm when the officer gave us the news. I was able to ask a few questions. I had had the whole night to mull over the idea that this young man could be André. Since I understood André's anguish and despair, I could conceive that he would have done this. The other members of my family, however, were completely taken aback. In that one tiny moment, their worlds shattered into a million pieces.

In the weeks and months following this tragedy, we experienced many conflicting emotions. It was like being on a rollercoaster ride. We went from incomprehension, to anger, to sadness. There were so many unanswered questions. How could André have done this to us? What had we done to him that he could carry out such an incomprehensible act? What could we or should we have done to prevent this tragedy? I remember one morning, waking up with tears running down my cheeks... a sign that this would certainly be another heartbreaking day.

Once the initial shock wore off, what I struggled with the most was to see the effect that this desperate act had on my husband and my two other children. They were experiencing a great deal of pain and distress. Not only had we lost a son or a brother but we had also lost all the precious moments we could have had with him. All our hopes and dreams for him vanished and our lives changed forever.

In the first few months, I was very angry that André had decided to end his life instead of trying to combat this illness. I had managed to fight the disease so why had he not done the same? My anger soon subsided and turned to great sorrow and sadness, as I knew what it meant to live with depression and that the road ahead for him would have been a very difficult and troubled one.

It seemed so tragic that someone with so much talent and potential could end his life in such a way. I often wonder what other good deeds André could have performed were he still with us.

It is always a dilemma to answer the question – How many children do you have? The first time someone asked this question, only days after the tragedy happened, my heart almost stopped beating. How am I supposed to answer such a question? To this day, I am still not sure how to answer it correctly....

I would love to be able to hold André in my arms, to see his beaming smile, but I no longer have this privilege. I can only hope that other families will find help in time in order to prevent another such tragedy.

Festival off to Hot Start

MARC GALLANT / WINNIPEG FREE PRESS

Playing with fire

Juggler Andre Dupont keeps his hands warm last night during the opening evening at the annual Festival du Voyageur, which runs until Feb. 23. For a sneak preview of this weekend's festival lineup, please see story on page **C**1.

My own treasure hunt begins...

Several events helped me to accept and be at peace with André's tragic death.

We received tremendous support from our families, friends, colleagues, and neighbours, as well as from André's many friends. The whole community rallied around us. We were swept away by a tidal wave of love. It was a life-changing experience to be the recipient of such an outpouring of love.

I see now that I, too, participated in a treasure hunt of sorts....

The picture that appears on the cover of this book was very consoling. In it, André is juggling with fire in front of an ice sculpture of a voyageur playing the fiddle. This picture appeared on the front page of our daily newspaper, the *Winnipeg Free Press*, to announce the start of the Festival du Voyageur in February 2003. The festival's mission is to commemorate the fur-trading era and inject some warmth and excitement into the middle of winter. André looked so happy in this picture!

I consider fire to be a symbol of healing and renewal. When I look at this picture, I see André going towards the light. I see that he brought this light into our lives for a very brief moment. He is also sharing that light with us, inviting us to help build a better world.

André's passion for life is also reflected in this picture.

The story, *Lost in the Storm*, which I found after his death, was yet another sign that helped me understand that my son is now happy and at peace. The suffering has ended. What more could I want for him?

The picture of André juggling with fire and the story that he wrote as a child, helped me understand what had happened to him. André is the one who helped me make sense of it all.

In France

The Louise Bridge in Winnipeg, Manitoba

I make some intriguing discoveries...

As André was growing up, I thought and hoped that some day he might become an architect or geologist. He loved to pore over books about old buildings and grand structures. He also had a keen interest in geography and, as a teenager, loved to explore his surroundings. As I was going through his photo albums after his death, two pictures caught my eye.

The picture of André in front of the sign "Ville du Pont" in France and the one taken by the Louise Bridge (Le pont Louise) in Winnipeg are clues that make me think that André wanted me to be a bridge between the life he once led on Earth and the life he now leads. My name is Louise Dupont, after all!

I do not see death as the end anymore. I see it as a transition towards another world or realm. Some time after André's death, a friend told me that I would always have a relationship with my son but that it would simply be of a different kind. In fact, I do have a good relationship with André, but it is true that it is very different from what it once was.

Bridges are powerful symbols that speak to us of going from one place to another or moving from one stage to another. This tragic event was a catalyst or bridge that allowed me to reaffirm my belief in a loving presence that sustained me throughout this very challenging time in my life.

André is no longer physically present but he is certainly present in my heart. He continues to inspire me. I believe we have come to this Earth to learn to detach ourselves from the material and physical aspects of our lives, as well as to learn to detach from our past failures and worries about the future. We are meant to learn to live in the present moment. I invite you to look for clues in the story *Lost in the Storm* and throughout the book to discover the messages related to these themes.

When I first started writing this book, I wanted to share the messages I had found in the story *Lost in the Storm*. After a while, it occurred to me that this book could also be used to start a dialogue and reflection on suicide, depression and, most of all, dying. Our society does everything to discourage us from discussing these serious issues. We are encouraged to flee death at all costs.

After his death, people would comment on how much André had accomplished in such a short time. It was as if he knew that his stay on Earth would be very brief.

Writing this book helps me remember and honour his short passage here on Earth. He left us a rich heritage of messages, in both the story he wrote as a child and the actions he took to help others. Although André made the decision to leave us at a young age, I believe he would have wanted the loved ones that he left behind to live out their lives fully and consciously. I think it is fitting that his ashes are buried in the part of the cemetery called *The Garden of Memories*.

One of André's last actions still intrigues me. On the day of his death, before leaving us forever, he taught his younger brother Christian how to juggle with fire. What is the significance of this act? I believe André was passing the flame on to his brother, to me and to everyone who knew him.

I received many gifts...

I have always enjoyed writing. This tragedy has allowed me to do something I have always dreamed of doing: writing a book. We often hear that after a loss, one door closes but another one opens. This is in effect what has happened to me.

From the onset of this tragedy, everyone around us acted in such loving and compassionate ways. It was heartwarming to discover that my son had touched the lives of so many people. These are but a few examples of people's generosity....

We received hundreds of cards and messages and many visitors brought food or flowers. Our families, through their constant presence and generosity, supported us in many different ways.

One of my husband's former colleagues, as well as the staff from Greenview School in Edmonton, sent us a booklet of poems and prayers. It was a great comfort to know that people who did not even know us were thinking about us and praying for us. We were assigned to different prayer groups: the Society of the Little Flower, the Franciscan Friars of the Atonement, and the Sisters of the Cenacle. There are now hundreds of people praying for us all over the world.

Alain, a friend of André's from France, sent us a collage of photos and a huge bouquet of flowers. Later on, he sent me a poem that he had written about his Canadian friend.

André and his friend, Pascal, visiting with their friend, Alain, in France.

My colleagues at the St. Boniface Library did all that they could to make my return to work after André's death as easy as possible. There are no words to convey how touched and moved I was by their compassion and love. They knew exactly what to say and what to do to ease my pain. Library patrons were also very kind to me. One patron in particular would bring me a chocolate kiss when she came in every week.

We received a comforting letter from Hilda Wyenberg who worked for the Adult ESL Centre. She taught English to our Columbian friends, the Jimenez family. Here is an excerpt from her letter:

Your son was so good to this family. I'm not sure how to communicate to you how much he meant to them. They spoke of him very often to me, not only of how much he helped them in their day-to-day decisions, but of how much they enjoyed his friendship. André showed to them that they had friends here in Canada, that they would be accepted in their new country. Immigration is a very difficult process and very lonely in many respects. Your son broke through these challenges and opened many doors, both physically and emotionally, for this family.

At the family viewing, our friend Miguel, head of the Colombian family, kept vigil by my son's side. This was a profoundly moving experience. Here was a man who came from another continent, who had endured many hardships in his life, sitting by my son, watching and praying over him....

Some of Andre's close friends took a small amount of his ashes to Nopiming Provincial Park. This was such a precious gift because I know that this was one of Andre's favourite places.

For a while, André had hosted a radio program on Envol FM, a radio station for the French community in Manitoba. The program was called *A cat has ten fingers*. After his death, in April 2003, his friends dedicated two programs to him. Through these broadcasts, it was as if André was sending out this message to his audience:

Listen with your spirit, not with your ears.

Nopiming Provincial Park

Students offer comfort...

I was greatly consoled and comforted by the cards and drawings we received from the students of École Christine-Lespérance, where André worked as an educational assistant. The cards and drawings presented in this book and on the following pages are a sample of the cards we received.

Lord, welcome into your home, André, who has left us and whom we loved dearly.

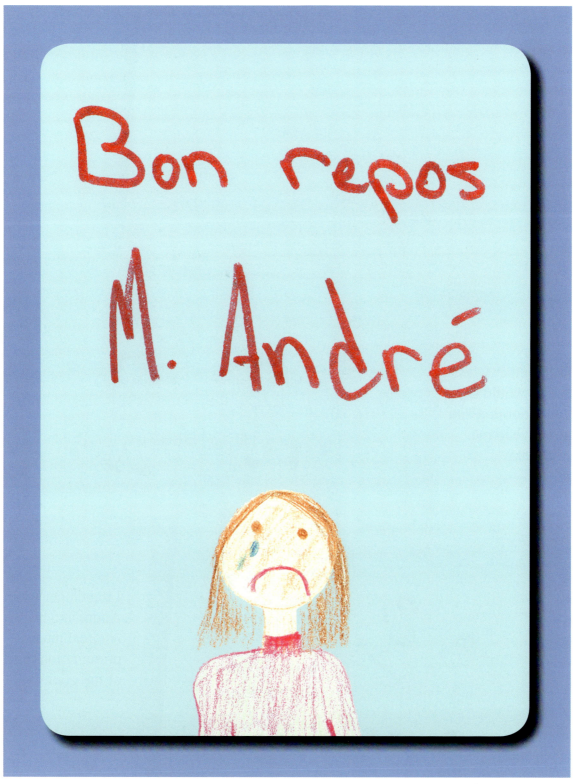

Have a good rest, Mr. André.

Marianne

My memories of André

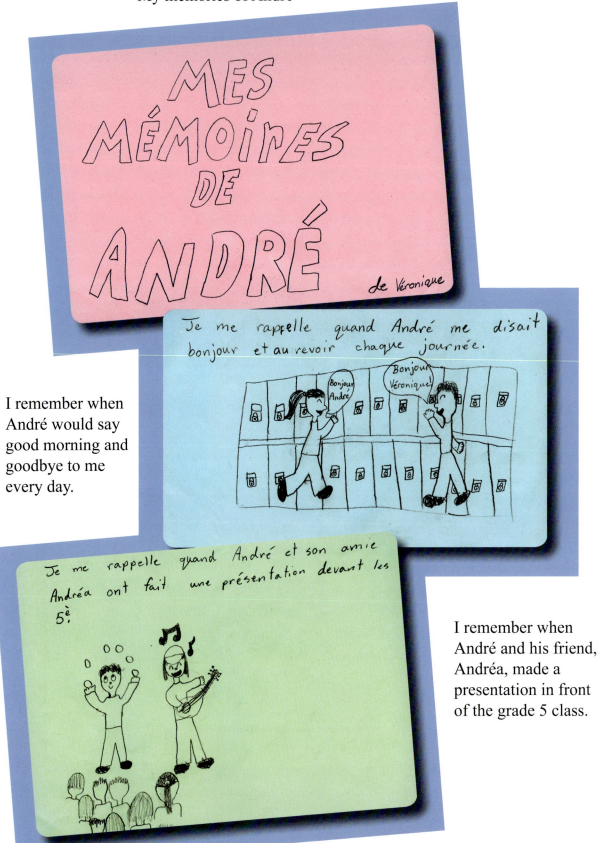

I remember when André would say good morning and goodbye to me every day.

I remember when André and his friend, Andréa, made a presentation in front of the grade 5 class.

May you be at rest in your pollution-free world. I remember how you hated all the pollution in the world. You always rode your bicycle. It's too bad that you died, but I will always remember you.

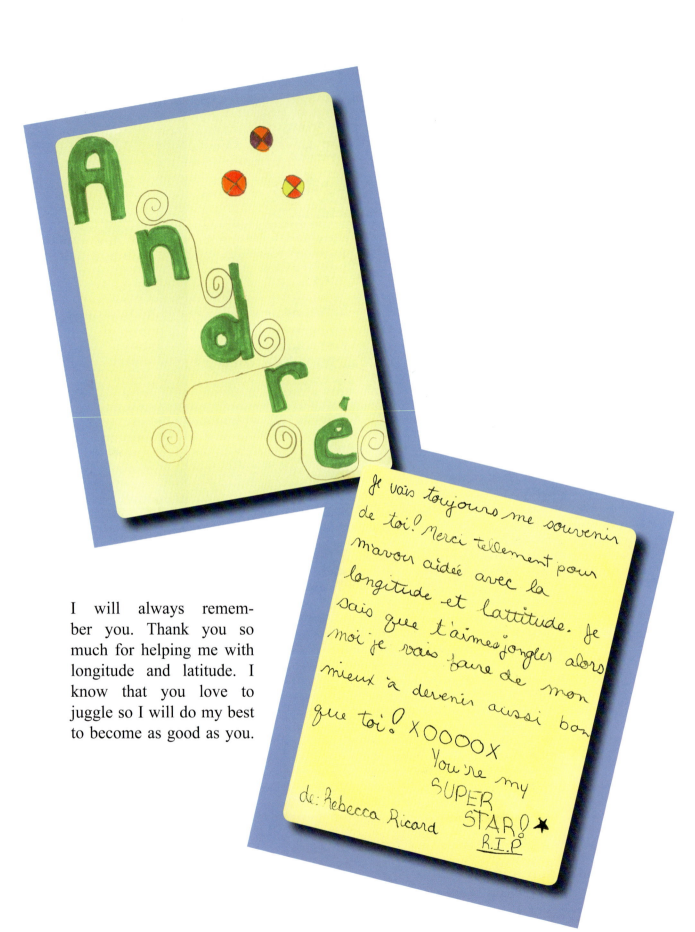

I will always remember you. Thank you so much for helping me with longitude and latitude. I know that you love to juggle so I will do my best to become as good as you.

André,
You were a very good juggler. You could juggle with almost anything you saw. You helped me when I had problems in class.

                                            I love you.

                                            Your friend,
                                            Justin

Daniel

For you, André...

Dear André...
I built you a paradise, so that you won't forget the moments from our past.

In my paradise there are flowers that laugh.

In my paradise there is a very happy sun.

And in my paradise there is all my love!

Photo : Janelle Potvin

LOUISE DUPONT
Author

louise.dupont1@live.com

Born in 1954, Louise Dupont worked for many years at the St. Boniface branch of the Winnipeg Public Library. She has always had a keen interest in spirituality and healing. As well as being cathartic, writing this book has given her the opportunity to explore these themes. This book was originally written in French and published in 2009.

All profits made from the sale of this book will be donated to non-profit organizations.

Here is a list of books that have helped and inspired me:

• *The Grief Recovery Handbook : The Action Program for Moving Beyond Death, Divorce, and Other Losses* / John W. James and Russell Friedman, HarperPerennial, 1998

• *Hannah's Gift : Lessons from a Life Fully Lived* / Maria Housden, Bantam Books, 2003

• *The Power of Now : A Guide to Spiritual Enlightenment* / Eckhart Tolle, Namaste Publishing, 1999

• *The Power of Intention : Learning to Co-create Your World Your Way* / Wayne W. Dyer, Hay House Inc., 2004

• *The Power of Your Subconscious Mind* / Joseph Murphy, PhD., D.D., Prentice Hall Press, 2008

Resources

If you or someone you know is contemplating suicide, there are people who can help.

IN MANITOBA, CALL:

Manitoba Suicide Line:
Toll free: 1-877-435-7170

Klinic's Crisis Line:
786-8686
Toll free: 1-888-322-3019

IN CANADA, VISIT:

The Canadian Mental Health Association
www.cmha.ca

FOR YOUTH AND TEENS, CALL OR VISIT:

Kids Help Phone
Toll-free: 1-800-668-6868
www.KidsHelpPhone.ca

Blue Wave Foundation
www.ok2bblue.com